The

Ex-Con Factor™

You Did Your Time, Now What?

Journey from D.O.C. to C.E.O.

By Tonia Quarterman
Foreword By Dr. Walter Sims

Willi,

No Matter what you've Been through you're still Some Good!

The EX-CON FACTOR™
You Did Your Time, Now What?
Journey from D.O.C. to C.E.O.
Copyright © 2016 by MQTQ ENTERPRISES LLC

All rights reserved. No part of this book may be reproduced or transmitted in any form or by any means without written permission from the author.

E-book:
ISBN: 978-0-9979222-0-2
ASIN: B01JPIZMSM

Paperback:
ISBN-10: 0997922214
ISBN-13: 978-0997922219

Published by MQTQ ENTERPRISES LLC

Table Of Contents

A letter to myself… .... - 5 -

Foreword .... - 6 -

Preface .... - 7 -

Introduction .... - 10 -

1 Hindsight 20/20 .... - 12 -

2 Ding Dong! Look Who's Home! .... - 14 -

3 Pack it up, you're going to prison! .... - 26 -

4 Sentenced to Read .... - 32 -

5 Mindset Reset .... - 37 -

6 Prison was easier .... - 44 -

7 Contraband Queen .... - 50 -

8 Inspiration Is Free .... - 56 -

9 Yeah, I Lied .... - 58 -

10 Drugs & Money .... - 64 -

11 Easy Money .... - 67 -

.12 Spending vs Investing .... - 70 -

13 Opportunity Under Your Nose .... - 76 -

14 Drop Dead .... - 80 -

15 Greatness is in You .... - 84 -

16 Mama's Baby, Daddy's Maybe .... - 87 -

17 No, Thank You! .... - 93 -

18 I got the keys, the keys, the keys .... - 98 -

19 Broke, Busted, & Disgusted? ....- 103 -

20 Seven Things I Wish I Knew as a Juvenile........- 106 -

21 Re-Entry Action List ....- 108 -

Stay in Touch & Support ....- 109 -

Become a book sponsor!...................................- 110 -

Coming Soon! ....- 111 -

Notes ....- 112 -

Action Plan ....- 113 -

Affirmations ....- 114 -

Contacts ....- 115 -

To Do List..- 116 -

A letter to myself…

Dear Ms. Mendoza,

First I want to apologize for judging you. You did what you did with what you had and what you knew at the time. I regret thinking less of you and being embarrassed by you. You really are my strength and all that my life experiences are based on. You are the reason I am such an intellectual today. Today I am finally grateful for everything you've taught me and done. You are an amazing and awesome person who adds value to me with your endurance and strength. You made a way out of a difficult path. Your choices crafted the masterpiece which is me.

*Love,
Tonia*

Foreword

People want to listen to and learn from people who have lived what they have written about. Tonia is that author who has lived what is between the pages of her book. She served her time and now she is serving as CEO of her own business. How did she do it? Well you have to read it to experience her journey. As you read this book, challenge yourself to become better. If Tonia can do it, you can do whatever you set your mind to do.

Dr. Walter Sims
The Minister of Motivation

Preface

The Ex-Con Factor, You Did Your Time Now What? Deals with the ex-con factor in particular, but the principles I will be talking about also deal with other ex-circumstances, situations or relationships with people, money and life. What qualifies me to talk about all these things? I feel like Melvin in the movie Baby Boy. "I been there and done it all to the full." If I haven't been there, I've seen it.

If you get in your feelings easily and aren't ready to actually do anything different, put this book down and come back when you're ready. I'm sure to step on some toes but it's ok. Put your steel toes on and let's keep it moving.

There are many people who follow the script and do what is considered right and go along to have a great uneventful life. (Because of me, my mother has several colorful holiday stories to share.) Then there are some who generally do what they're told. Something happens outside of their control, maybe they make a bad choice or end up in the wrong place at the wrong time. You live every day, not just once, so make the best of every day. Choices are for you to make and it's never too late to start making better ones.

I didn't follow the script in my life. I had every chance to make different decisions; there were even better opportunities for me that I didn't take advantage of. I have lived, learned and paid the price. This is why I don't like to make or take excuses. Yes, there's a factor but there are no excuses.

Introduction

Sharing some of my experiences and observations in this book in an effort to inspire someone to make better decisions. I'm educated, fabulous, cool to be around, tell it like it is, wife, mother, friend, business owner, home owner, member of the community and I was convicted of a felony in 1994. I'm not proud of the things I've done but all my decisions and experiences make me the person I am today who I am proud of. If not for that, I may just have been somewhere being average. Instead, I'm embracing the good, letting go of the bad, and sharing some of it with you. I hope my experiences make a positive impact in someone's life. If nothing else, I hope it makes someone think and think again before making a wrong move.

1 Hindsight 20/20

What if I…
- Wasn't attracted to the wrong type of men?
- Never smoked weed that first time?
- Quit him the first time he slapped me?
- Wasn't in love with fast money?
- Wasn't attracted to a fast lifestyle?
- Left him after he shot me?
- Never fought back?
- Never picked up that weapon?

All of this, before I was out of my teens…

Even though I was disfigured, disabled and disenfranchised at such an early age I can share this because I survived it. I now stand in a place of power and not a place of pain and recognize it was all tied to my destiny.

2 Ding Dong! Look Who's Home!

The day you have been waiting for is here! Finally, you're home. Everyone is glad to see you and you couldn't be happier. Maybe there's a barbecue waiting for you, or a block party. Or maybe, just close family and friends stopping by to see you, or to come scoop you up to go get a drink or something of that nature. Either way, you're free, and have a chance to stay free. Of course everyone wants to see their friends and family. This is your chance for a fresh start. Don't get caught up in the celebration. There's much that you need to do when you first get home to be successful. If you're on probation you want to go and report as soon as possible.

I am a "business first" thinker. Before the celebrations begin, think before you act. Your actions affect more than just you. Before you put your freedom in jeopardy, think about those who took care of you while you were incarcerated. Those who sent you money, accepted your phone calls, and visited you. Those who had the daunting and emotional task of bringing your children to see you. The person who had the job of answering those tough questions your children surely had on your behalf. When the fact is you had three hots and a cot, and they were out in the real world working and helping take care of you and yours.

I'm grateful that when I went to prison, I didn't have any children. One of the saddest things to witness, was a mother who hasn't seen her children in months, or even years, because she had no one to bring them. I was fortunate to have family and friends that supported me with calls, visits and kept me at mail call. I really appreciate that support and I realize that no one had to stick with me.

I can definitely say because of my family, I now make better decisions, check my temper, and do my best to stay out of foolishness. I'm not saying that it doesn't come my way, however, I now understand what I actually stand to lose… everything. Nothing is worth your life or your freedom.

What types of things jeopardize your freedom? Child support? Sometimes dealing with the court with civil and family matters can bring on great anxiety. Go ahead and get the help you need. Sometimes all you have to do is ask a clerk, fill out some papers (sometimes a thick stack) and file them.

Do you have a problem completing probation? Could it be you're spending time with the wrong crowd? Or seems like you're always in the wrong place at the wrong time? Traffic tickets? Or driving with no license or suspended or revoked? I violated probation and house arrest so many times it was ridiculous. Worse, it was usually with a new charge. Being hard headed and wild was my way of life.

Domestic violence? Are you simply with the wrong person? Sometimes people bring out the worst in you and it's up to you to change your environment. Or it could just be you! Maybe you have a bad temper? There's help with counseling for coping skills and dealing with your emotions. Do you pop off or do things without thinking about possible consequences? What can you do to change these things?

What did you say you would do when you got home? Did you find religion in prison? Did you learn a trade or get a degree? Did you get your GED? Surely you made some promises to yourself and others before you came home. Whatever your promises were, do you plan to stick to them? There are many that have good intentions that go out the window as soon as your feet hit the ground. It may take a day, week, month or a couple of months. Many times this because you insert yourself back into familiar surroundings, without a real plan. Sometimes you try your best and things just don't go the way you think they should.

You may need to get a new ID or driver's license. In my case I had to reinstate my license, because my tag needed to be turned in while I was in prison resulting in a suspended license. This brought the cost of a new license from $25 up to $125 plus the cost for insurance. For someone just jumping out, small setbacks like this can seem overwhelming. It might seem easier to go back to what you know (illegal activity) *just to get on my feet.*

Since everyone doesn't go to prison

for the same thing I can't say there's any one magic pill to ensure, not going down the same road. One thing is for certain, you always have a choice.

Thankfully, I was sent to a work-release center to get a head start on returning to the "free world".

Only the excitement that I felt at the idea of work release quickly dissipated when reality kicked in. Explaining to every job I applied to, that I was in a work release center (and of course they wanted to know why) became emotionally draining.

I absolutely understand the struggle. *If you're in the position to hire someone who has been incarcerated use your discretion, but don't just count people out. Everyone knows someone who has been in some kind of trouble. I don't know if people are afraid, judgmental, or just ignorant.*

Some people who have been to prison are the best employees you can have. You'd have to hire one first to find out. I'm not saying to just hire someone who is not qualified or who isn't a good fit but in my experience the actual event that led me to prison could have been anyone's daughter. The bottom line is, things happen, and split second decisions can change your life forever.

Just a few weeks after my 19th birthday I was on the news, with a first degree felony. In my ignorance, I didn't know I should have plead self-defense. I remember the detective asking me over and over if I was afraid for my life. I didn't know those were the magic words. I just told them what happened and I really was just in complete shock. Ignorance is very expensive. I paid with my freedom, my right to vote, my right to bear arms. The state makes it very difficult for you to be made whole again, if ever, even once your sentence is complete. Especially in Florida which is my personal experience.

I started the process as soon as I completed my sentence. It will take patience and perseverance to get these things done. It took me a long time and what I think was a big runaround to get my civil rights restored. Sometimes I'd swear I was talking to someone from back in the 1950's with a manual typewriter and fans blowing in their office, the way they acted like they are so backlogged. I say "acted" because the process should be automatic but Florida's antiquated, ways need to be updated.

Everything about the prison system reminds me of slave movies. I remained diligent through the state's changing procedures which actually set me back several years. There's paperwork there right now that's been in Tallahassee since 2007. Even though I've completed my sentence, probation, & paid thousands in restitution the state specifically kept my firearm authority. I had to apply for that separately. I guess no one has had time to make a decision on it up to now in 2016. After having my rights restored in 2005, 9 years after being released from prison, and 4 years after completing all the requirements. I was finally able to vote for the first time ever. I don't know if my vote counts or not but I'm exercising my right. We have to start somewhere and I figure I can't whine about the way things are if I don't at least go vote. Take advantage of absentee ballots if you don't want to go stand in line at the polls. Also note that your local elections are where the changes that apply to you are generally made. Don't just concentrate on the Presidential elections.

It may seem unfair but, in order to win you have to play by their rules. So learn their rules, then do what you have to do.

3 Pack it up, you're going to prison!

Mendoza! Pack it up you're going to prison! Another inmate yelled at about 4:15 a.m. two weeks after I was sentenced to five years D.O.C. I jumped out of that bunk so fast. And proceeded to *"pack it up"*. I was ready to go do this time since time in the county jail is considered *dead time*. Meaning, it's generally counted day for day instead of earning gain time or time for good behavior.

I remember one notorious inmate who was sentenced to Florida's Death Row telling me I'd be waiting for a long time to get sentenced and then another long time to get sent to prison because that was her experience. Well, everyone's situation is different and it's best not to get sucked in to jail house chatter. It only makes you fear the unknown.

"Who'd think in elementary, hey I'd see the penitentiary?" ~ Tupac Shakur

I bet you are still wondering, what did this girl do? My activities included selling drugs, wasting time, running the street and being involved with anything that wasn't right. I spent a lot of time being a lost soul. Have you ever been somewhere and felt like you were out of your element?

I survived more than one abusive and destructive relationships. I've watched domestic violence since I was a child and I always said it would not be me, but it was.

I never went looking for trouble and didn't bother anyone. I minded my business and made my money. I never really had too many problems with people in the streets because I respected everybody. The problems were in personal relationships.

Domestic violence starts a lot earlier than many people realize and can become a recurring cycle. My next book "Keep Your Hands to Yourself" will delve deeper into this subject. At 17 years old I was shot with a 12gauge shotgun by my boyfriend. He was charged with negligence but the fact that the gun was even pointed at me showed a lack of respect. I think we fought every day! Between smoking, drinking, partying, my slick mouth and me refusing to let someone put their hands on me was a recipe for disaster. By the time I was in my next relationship I was pretty seasoned at fighting back. At 19 years old I was with someone else who was abusive and that relationship ended with me charged with second-degree murder.

4 Sentenced to Read

During the writing of this book a breakthrough happened on the way from Atlanta with a friend. Understand that in order to share all this with you I had to forgive myself and realize that all that I've been through wasn't about me. I have to share my experiences and lessons to hopefully help someone else. I really didn't know my worth back then and sometimes now I still have to remind myself. The new me had to stop judging the old me for my bad decisions. Because of these bad decisions I am able to share the what not to do because, I've done so many things the wrong way.Even with the ridiculous decisions that I had been making for my life I still managed to stay in some kind of educational program, granted, some were court ordered. As a juvenile I was always sentenced to programs like "Sentenced to Read", a GED prep program. It seems like people may have seen something in me that I had not yet recognized in myself. While receiving college acceptance letters in the mail I was being arraigned for second degree murder and looking at 20 years in prison. I never thought that I would see the light of day again.

Just like the first time I ever got in trouble when I took my grandmother's car at 15 years old I never knew that there was such a thing as juvenile detention I thought I was going straight to the 33rd ST. jail.

Juvenile was a playhouse of sorts I met so many "friends" that I never knew before and all the problems that my family was trying to warn me about. Of course I didn't want to hear it, I knew everything and wanted to do whatever I felt like. I was so lost. Juvenile was goons in training and it was co-ed so it was all good. I met everybody who knew everything crooked. I was now in cahoots with everyone who knew how to steal a car, sell drugs, rob, steal and worse. I believe the worst I had done before being exposed to this may have been stay out late at the *Funtastic* skating ring, smoke a joint or drink. This was the late 80s and there was plenty of money to be made and I was all over it.

From the first time I went, I continued to violate probation based on my choices. My grandmother felt guilty for calling the police that day when they carted me off the first time. I'm sure it broke her heart to see me handcuffed and taken away. When I got older, I told her not to feel bad because I realized it was my choices that got me put back in there over and over again. I didn't want to abide by the rules. She told me if I would just go to school she would buy me a car and pay for college if I would "just leave the boys alone". Well, needless to say, that didn't happen. I seemed to go for the worst of the worst. I came from a good home and family, but I chose the streets.

There was a certain type of lifestyle that excited me. Truth be told it still excites me today, but my freedom is more important to me today than ever.

I think there's one thing that is more addicting than using drugs, it's selling them. "Nothing like that iron"...but I've realized you can't live any kind of life behind bars. There is no sense being a king or queen pin in the pen. My mindset has since changed. I've changed the product but not the hustle. Pair all that with some education, a real "WHY" and common sense, this gives you a recipe for success.

5 Mindset Reset

"You can't be who you're going to be and who you used to be at the same time!" ~T.D. Jakes

I certainly wasn't going to be cutting grass and chopping down trees on the outside, but wait a minute, hell, I was doing that for free on the inside hmm…. Seems like my mindset needed adjusting.

I must say prison was a humbling experience. It helped me to realize that I would do what I had to do to remain free because they definitely have somewhere for people who can't get right or those who just won't get right. I see so many friends, relatives, and acquaintances that continued to go back to prison. I understand wholeheartedly the hardships and difficulties that come along with being an ex-con. However just like the things that got you into prison were choice it is also a decision to remain free. Yes, there is an ex-con factor but there are no excuses. The fact is I had plenty of experience in sales, leadership, hustling, I had the wherewithal to get up early in the morning and stay up all night at a trap house so I could definitely work first second or third shift slinging waffles.

What do you mean you can't work night shift? What do you mean it's too early in the morning? Didn't you get up every day in prison make your bed sweep, mop and buff their floors, cook their food, cut their grass, eat, sleep, shit when they told you to for free? Don't even get me started on the work detail where they make extra money off of you. That is the new slavery.

Any excuse that you had not to work while incarcerated would get your behind locked up inside of the lockup. What is going on so great that you can't work or do whatever is required of you in the free world? Don't be a fool!

It doesn't matter if you were making $1 million or a hundred million before you were incarcerated, change some of that knowledge that you used to make that million and gear it toward something positive. You have CEO potential and being the CEO of your life is the best job ever. At least you won't have to be looking over your shoulders at every turn. I'm just grateful to still be here in spite of all the crazy situations I put myself in. I can only shake my head at myself now. I am so cautious now, but I obviously didn't give a damn back then.

When I got to Lowell, I remember the intake process feeling apprehensive because I had been to jail but never to prison. When going to classification I made sure to act like I had some sense so that I wouldn't get sent to the kiddie dorm. That's where the younger inmates were who didn't mind blowing or extending yours/their time with foolishness. By this time, I had just turned 21 years old and although I was still on the wild side, I just wanted to do my time and go home.

It worked, and I was sent to Forest Hills. This was a camp with no fence for inmates who met certain criteria. The other inmates on the main compound called us the "Golden Girls" because of the yellow dresses we had to wear and the privileges being at the minimum security camp.

I worked for 60 days on the inside grounds job detail until I was able to get a transfer. Thankfully I got transferred to a vocation.

Use what you know and monetize it. If it's cooking, cleaning, fixing things use it! No excuses! I know many people wash and iron clothes in prison to survive but wouldn't do it on the outside to remain free what kind of sense does that make? I respect that kind of hustle.

Are you an artist? Can you cut hair? Some professions are barber, tattoo artist, make custom designs for cars, clothes etcetera.

Perfect your craft, get a business license and do your thing. There are classes at your local community college to make it official. Take your natural talent to the next level. I find that some people just want to do what comes easily. There are so many talented individuals with so much potential but they don't want to go get technical training because they're not good at math or reading. That's what remedial classes are for.

Any chance you get to enhance your skillset, take it. I'm convinced, I can do anything!

The future kind of looked bright for me when I got out… but who knew no one would want to hire a felon?

6 Prison was easier

I had been at the work release center for 30 days. Literally pounding the pavement and spilling my guts to the potential employers who wanted to know what a pretty girl like me was doing in prison.

The catch was, inmates had 45 days to find a job or they placed you at a local nursery to work for minimum wage or you go back to prison. Well at this point, prison didn't sound too bad. Even though while in prison I couldn't wait for the privilege to go to work release, however, this was beginning to be a harder transition than I could have imagined. Moreover, while in prison I was getting 20 days a month in gain time compared to work release where 12 days a month was the maximum, a fact which essentially lengthened my time.

At this point I was frustrated and tired of reliving the incident which had resulted in my prison stay. During visitation one Saturday, my grandmother and her friend came to see me. I informed her of my decision to tell the powers that be to send me back to prison! That work release was too hard made no sense. How could I live in society when I couldn't even get a job? I mean no one would hire me! Of course I could just go back to prison, complete my sentence, get out and go back to life as I knew it. A fast life, fast money, by any means necessary and then continue the cycle in the revolving door of recidivism. How grateful I am to have a praying grandmother! She and her friend prayed fervently that day with me in the visiting park at the picnic table. They declared that I would have a job by Monday! "Alright" I said, "If you say so Mommy Darling" as I kissed her good-bye.

The following Monday I commenced the ritual of getting dressed, walking to the bus stop and pounding the pavement, filling out applications and asking local businesses if they were hiring.

While in prison along with working in the garden, cutting grass and maintaining the grounds I also had a chance to learn a couple of vocations. I was certified in tailoring and alterations and I also earned a certificate in business administration. This was another area of favor in my life because inmates in state corrections are supposed to go from work detail to vocation then back to work detail. I was granted the privilege of going from vocation to vocation which I was very grateful for. If I could avoid working out in the hot sun, then by all means I would. However, I am grateful today for those experiences because it lets me know that against all odds I can do anything I have to do to survive.

If your mindset is right, you'll never go hungry, and hopefully stay free in the process.

See, the first year of being in prison my mindset was still the same. I had planned to get out, get a package and get back on my grind. Selling drugs and other illegal activity was the most exciting lifestyle to me and since that was not what landed me in prison I thought it was the way to go.

Eventually, actually about a year into my sentence, I realized I was working in prison for free, every day. Why couldn't I just get a job on the outside? It didn't matter what I was doing because after arriving to Lowell and completing R&O (reception & orientation) I was put on inside grounds for work detail. For me this was hell on earth! Outdoors with rows upon rows of peas to pick! Acres of grass to cut, forests of pine trees to trim with pick axes! I thought I had been dropped back off into slavery days! I mean we used to sing old Negro spirituals and all on the work truck in the morning. They handed me a five-gallon bucket and told me to fill it, out in the hot ass sun! I remember thinking I was going to die out here. I just turned the bucket upside down and sat on it holding my head. I was thinking, lord, I have five years what the hell am I going to do? This is some bullshit!

7 Contraband Queen

It took a while for me to change my thinking. It's safe to say part of my personality is I always wanted to push things to the limit. One of the sergeant's nicknamed me the "Contraband Queen". Not for anything dangerous but just things to make my life more comfortable. For example, if I could get extra boxes sent in under someone else's name I would do it. Then I'd have to explain how I had several extra pairs of shoes, jewelry, toiletries etcetera.

Some of the correctional officers were cool and just were regular people who came to work to do their eight and hit the gate. Others were butt holes that seemed to live to make your life miserable. One day I complimented a

Lieutenant on her hairstyle and asked her what it was called. The heifer told me "if you stayed out of prison you'd know what it's called." I laughed then and I can still laugh about it now. The nerve of her. But she was right. I think I also asked her when I was going to work release and she told me to get out of her face. (It was the next morning!)

While out job hunting, I had to call the work release center to check in every hour. I was told to come back to the center because there's a company that wants to interview me. Waffle House. I had never applied there but I made my way back to the center. Turns out another inmate had applied there months before, but she was already employed by now and they were just calling to see if anyone needed a job. Well this day another inmate had quit her job on a construction site so they sent the two of us out on this interview. I was so nervous. I never thought I could be a waitress, remember I had gotten shot in my shoulder and I had always pictured waitresses carrying these huge trays which I would not be able to do. At least not without everything being on the floor on a regular basis. We both interviewed, and I got the job! On Monday! Just like my grandmother said!

 She really didn't like me working there, she said it wasn't prestigious enough. I was fine with it at the time because of where my skillset was. I knew Hustlenomics 101 but that really wasn't a marketable skill. I learned a lot about customer service and developed my people skills while waiting tables. It also got me over my initial terror of yelling out orders in front of a restaurant full of people!

"Waffle! Order scrambled cheese raisin plate scattered, smothered, covered, chunked, one sausage!"

I waited tables for many years discouraged, thinking that no one else would hire me and it didn't matter if I had a PhD I would still have to check the "yes" box on job applications. My record couldn't be expunged because for now it's on the list that Florida has barred from expungement. Not saying that it shouldn't be, but it shouldn't be a blanket rule. Each case is different and should be considered individually before making everything a perpetual life sentence.

The bottom line is, prison was easier than figuring out life as a convict, but my freedom is worth the adversity.

Whether I agree with the rules or not, I am still grateful, because without these adversities I wouldn't be creating these opportunities and I am still GREAT!

8 Inspiration Is Free

I met my husband two weeks after getting out of prison. He will tell you what a rough customer I was. He said I was way too pretty to be so rough. He must have liked it because he put a ring on it. Two years later, we got married and a few years after started our family. This inspired me to go back to school. So I went to technical school and took up accounting. I acquired many more marketable skills but in the back of my mind I was wondering how it was all going to pan out. I was not alone in this either. Most of the ladies in the class with me had the same issues. Some kind of background issue that kept them from gaining employment in the fields we were learning. Here we were, willing to work, gaining the necessary tools but no one wanted to hire us.

I have to admit that I went to technical school first to avoid doing all those extra academics like science and history but while learning accounting a 65-year-old lady who just got her degree came in to speak to our class and inspired me to continue to complete my degree. If she could do it, so could I. Eventually I went ahead and took all the remedial math that I needed (I'm convinced algebra is the devil) and went on with my studies. The longest way anywhere is with a shortcut. I found this out with my schooling. It wouldn't have taken me nearly as long if I would have just went ahead and not avoided it for so long.

9 Yeah, I Lied

"It is easier to ask for forgiveness, than it is to get permission." ~ Grace Hopper

I got jobs in my field but only when I checked no! Ha! Who wants to live like that? I kept working at Waffle House part time and took accounting jobs through a temp agency until a permanent position came up.

When looking for part time I ended up with a full time position because the lady whom I was replacing was going out to have a baby and not coming back. I trained for the job for a little over three months. Only problem was that I would have to fill out a new application and pass a real background check. Well, I checked no in that dreaded "Have you ever been convicted" box and packed my belongings at my desk and worried for a whole week which seemed like an eternity.

My stuff was packed I was just waiting for that axe to drop. Every day I was wondering what was next. Finally, a call from HR. "do you have somewhere we can talk" I said "sure I will step outside and call you from my cellphone". The conversation went sort of like this...

HR: "Well everything was good but this one thing came up under Tonia Me-

ME: (I cut her off) I said "yeah that's me" (The charge was under my maiden name.)

HR: "Would you like to tell me more about it?"

ME: "No, not if it's not going to help me get the job."

HR: "I can see it was probably something very traumatic and I wouldn't want you to have to relive it again. But the problem is that you checked "no" on the application."

ME: (fast talking) "Well I received clemency from the Governor, I can vote and sit on a jury so I thought I could finally check no. I have a copy of it would you like me to fax it to you?" (I had just received it about 8 months before.)

HR: "Yes. That would be helpful but I can't promise anything."

I don't know what she said to who but I ended up getting the job and working there for three years until the economy crashed.

I knew I wasn't right for me to check that box. But I grew tired of the automatic "no's". I had to prove that I was qualified and could produce the same or better results as someone who wasn't burdened with a tainted past.

Lucky for me while I was working there I was still going to school taking one or two classes at a time so when I got laid off I just picked up a full schedule of school.

It took a total of nine years to get that four-year degree but I did it. No one can take it away. Don't think that it's something you can't do because it's been a long time since you've been in school. Like I've said before you have to start somewhere. The reasons you would be doing it now will be different than back when you had to try to fit in or deal with other things that school age children have to deal with. Incidentally, now your WHY is more relevant to the rest of your life and the road has more bumps.

I had to take remedial math and took about three tries to pass college algebra! What if I would have given up? My education coupled with my ambition has me of the mindset not to even ask for a J.O.B. (Just Over Broke) but to CREATE my own opportunities! I can't stop and I won't stop! Now Hustlenomics 101, Accounting & Business Makes me the CEO of being ME! Nothing against any of the occupations that I've had because I am so grateful for ALL my experiences but I know now that there's so much more for me to do! I had to share all this with you in hopes to let you know that you are enough! If I can do it so can you! I've been through more than what's in these pages some because of my own decisions and some not. I could have been dead so many times but I'm not. I've put myself in places and situations that still have me in awe sometimes. Sometimes I wonder where I found my fearlessness! I will say now that I redirect that energy into positive places and things. I was spared because there's a purpose on my life as there is for yours.

10 Drugs & Money

I had an opportunity to go back to the town I had got in trouble in but I chose to stay where I had my job when released from prison. It was a conscious decision, because I knew moving back would be a recipe for trouble. The fact is, everyone knew me and knew what type of things I was involved in. It's way too easy to get sucked back in.

In prison and work release they had us do mandatory drug treatment whether you were on drugs or not. I thought it was the stupidest thing ever because I wasn't addicted to drugs. I partied but never did anything that I couldn't give up. However, I did find out what I was addicted to. Money. If you're talking about getting some money I'm about that life. The drug treatment also gave me a different level of empathy that I didn't have before for people who were addicted to drugs. When you sell drugs you don't think about all the collateral damage that happens. I didn't care if someone sold all their food stamps or if their electricity was off. That wasn't my problem.

My attitude was, if they didn't buy from me they'd buy from someone else. Now I know that I'd rather be a part of the solution instead of part of the problem. I've learned to care more about people even if they don't care about themselves at the time. Today it's ok for me to walk away from being a part of that. In doing so I have come to a place of self respect and integrity.

11 Easy Money

One thing I've found is that easy money will ruin some people. So many dope boys don't want to work even when they do get out the game and start their own businesses. It takes the same, if not more tenacity, dedication and hard work to be successful. The rewards and peace of mind is unmatched.

I have three tips for people to be the best you can be:

1. Handle your business.
2. Handle your business.
3. Handle your business.

A job is a start but if you can start a business there's nothing like being your own boss.

Some people don't have the will to be an entrepreneur. That's all fine, I'm not knocking that. If I never had these adversities, I may have chosen that route. There are some things that need to be addressed if you start your own business.

Like everything else, learn your business and do it right. It's ok to learn along the way as long as you implement what you learn. I implore you not to be half assed. Also remember what goes around comes around so starting a bootleg business or selling things that fell off the back of the truck is not good karma.

If you have any kind of business, warranty your equipment. Invest in insurance. Insure yourself, your business, equipment and family. I hear people say they can't afford insurance but really in order to be successful and protect your livelihood, you can't afford not to.

Maintain your equipment and warranties. You can't make money when your bank accounts, equipment, websites etcetera are down.

Anticipate your needs for the future. Criminals live day to day, responsible people plan for the future.

Clean up your personal credit. Pull your credit report and dispute any incorrect information. Everyone gets a free credit report every year from annualcreditreport.com Use Credit Karma to watch your FICO scores for free.

Build business credit. If you don't know how, educate yourself. There are

several courses, workshops, books, Google and YouTube videos for everything under the sun.
- Invest in yourself, you're the best thing going. Invest in coaching or a class that you can elevate yourself.
- Take responsibility for your actions, credit, record, and overall situation.
- Never stop learning.

•

12 Spending vs Investing
Don't spend time in prison, invest it.
~Tonia Quarterman

There may not be another time in life when you will have nothing but time on your hands. Use this time wisely. With no one to care for or to look after but yourself this is the time to get YOU together. Even if it is making detailed plans on what you're going to do and how you're going to do it. I am not talking about thinking of a new harebrained schemes on how not to get caught or how to get the least amount of time on your next criminal endeavor.

If your credit is jacked up, start learning how to fix it. License messed up? Take the steps to get it right. Child support piling up? Use the law library to figure out how to do a modification, file for visitation rights too while you're at it. Just because you have to pay child support, visitation is not always included. You have to start somewhere. Even though you may run into obstacles don't give up. There will be hoops to jump through and if you keep a clear mind you can do it.

I had to stop smoking weed too. If I told you I did everything right since I've been out, I'd be lying through my teeth. I had a dirty pee test and couple of them that barely made it through which had the probation officer looking at me sideways asking what I did to it.

On one occasion he was so happy because I was doing so well towing the line working and paying the restitution but I was still burning a fatty every chance I got. I would literally leave the probation office and pull my pre-rolled blunt down off my visor and fire it up while pulling off from their office. I would have to curb my smoking before the next visit, but that free paper soon burned!

When that man let me slide and told me don't come back in here like that again, I didn't! I got a flashback and thought about how well I was doing and how utterly stupid it would have been for me to violate probation and get sent back to prison to work for free because I wanted to smoke weed. If I told you I didn't hustle at all I'd be lying too. But it was never the main thing and I don't recommend it. The grace that I was given I didn't take for granted. There's a way to do everything and if you know you're not doing right all I'm saying is, don't be careless or stupid. You've probably been gone a long time and things change. I can only shake my head when I see people still hang out on corners or at the store. Not on the corner man! Change the product, not the hustle.

Education is key. If you don't have your GED, get it. No excuses. The more education you have the better your chances of making a better life for yourself. However, if you're already educated it's going to take a mindset shift to deal with all the rest of the educated people who feel some type of way about working with a felon.

For the record, they're not better than you, they're just one bad decision away from what you've experienced. Either that or they haven't gotten caught.

13 Opportunity Under Your Nose

What do you already know how to do? There has to be something that you do well. Perfect your craft, learn your business and invest in yourself. You're the best thing going. Yes, you may have to work at a crappy job for a little while but it's what you do with your spare time that will show and tell what's important to you. Invest in a coach or class that can help you. Read, watch YouTube and learn all you can about what you want to do. Then implement it! There are college courses and funds available for you to go to school and learn a trade or get a degree. Check with your local career center for information on training opportunities. The career center can help you with resume writing and interview skills. They may or may not be able to lead you to a job but it's a place to start. I will be honest; they weren't much help for me because they said I was already doing well. That wasn't good enough for me! What was I to do if I wanted more? I've found that if no one will give you a job sometimes you just have to create one for yourself. I had created an additional stream of income making flower arrangements and gift baskets. It even flourished into a contract with a local furniture store for me to make all the arrangements for their showroom. I was also able to furnish our first home with the barter system. Don't sleep on the barter system. It is great when you are able to give value for value.

It pays to develop your people skills and network. When they say your network determines your net worth it is true. Your income will be close to the five closest people in your circle. Evaluate who you're spending your time with.

The lady that showed me the gift basket and flower arranging business was a customer of mine from the Waffle House. She and her husband came in for coffee every day and invited my husband and I over for drinks. She showed me the ins and outs of the business and how to charge for my work I went and got a business license and resale permit and Tonia's Floral Designs was born! I made more money doing that than working on the job all day.

Don't sleep on your passion. Always be working towards getting paid to do what you'd do for free.

Now, let's be realistic. If your background consists of fraud on the elderly, for example, don't go trying to be a CNA at a nursing home. Always look for the reality of getting employment in the field and what the real requirements are in the job market. So many people go to school and take loans to get certifications that they can't use because you need two years' experience straight out of school. Use common sense and get something that you will benefit from.

14 Drop Dead

I dropped out of school in the 10th grade for no other reason but that I was just hard headed as hell and at the time I could. Between getting in trouble, juvenile, and a dysfunctional relationship I managed to still get my GED at 18 anyway because my boyfriend was in jail and I had time to concentrate. Day two, the final day of the test, he was getting out but I made it my business to get up there and take that test. Plus, I think it was a condition of my probation at the time or something. I don't really remember but I'm glad I did it.

Do you have people in your life that are distractions? That you get caught up in their madness to where you can't concentrate on your own best interest and well-being? Maybe it's time to start recognizing who these people are, then push the delete button on them out of your life. I understand that some people are black holes that consume you and all your time. These are usually negative people who aren't going anywhere in life. I get this uneasy feeling anytime I'm around people that I feel like are wasting time. Worse… wasting my time. Just stand up and walk away. Your time is your most valuable asset.

A recent episode of Scandal, Olivia Pope told Jake to just stand up and walk out the door with her and he would be free. Now Jake thought he was going to get his brains blown out if he got up and left. When he took the chance and stood up, grabbed Olivia's hand, and walked out the door to freedom, it was a powerful and liberating scene

That is what you have to do sometimes with people who are not going anywhere in life. It doesn't matter if you have been around them all your life. I know you've heard the saying "if you want something different you have to do something different". Family, friends, it doesn't matter. You don't owe anyone anything. I repeat, you don't owe anyone anything. Likewise, they don't owe you anything. If you keep going back to jail or prison no one owes you anything. No one has to take care of you, no one has to send you commissary money no one has to come and visit you, no one has to accept your phone calls and no one has to write. Count yourself blessed if you do have someone that continues to support you through your foolishness.

I find that if we learn to take responsibility for our own actions we tend to make better decisions. Knowing that I made bad decisions and paid for them makes me have little sympathy for excuses. I don't like to make them or listen to them. Drop dead situations, and relationships and leave them where they are.

15 Greatness is in You
I ain't gonna beg you to be great.
~Tonia Quarterman

People say I make it sound so easy. I make it look easy because it is! When you look at it logically instead of emotionally it's easier to put things in perspective. Get out of your feelings! For real, when it comes down to doing what has to be done it can't be an emotional decision. I know it hurts to leave people and situations behind but do what you have to do to pull yourself up and out. In order to elevate sometimes you have to separate. I know for fact that it doesn't matter how much money you make you can still be successful based on your choices. It depends on what you make a priority. If smoking, drinking, hanging out, buying unnecessary items, or blowing money is more important to you than paying your bills, buying a home, paying your child support, paying restitution, student loans or probation cost then maybe you are not ready to do what it takes.

Don't do what you can, do what it takes. It helps to have someone on your side that is on the same page with your goals and aspirations. If you have good credit and a job you can pretty much get whatever you want. Remember it's not how much money you make, it's what you do with that money.

Even with the best intentions life happens. Always do the best you can to be a good steward over what you have. Especially things or money that belongs to other people like your credit for example. I have had help along the way. I don't play with people's money because I don't want anyone playing with mine. For example, don't be one of those people who uses someone else's credit but doesn't pay it back or whatever you have in their name you don't make it a priority.

If you owe someone pay them first. They didn't have to help you. Don't be a bum. Don't be one of those people that people regret helping. Call them first, don't make them run you down. Remember to run them down to pay them the same way you ran them down to borrow.

16 Mama's Baby, Daddy's Maybe

Going to jail about child support is crazy in my opinion. You can't make money in jail. Although if you handled your business all would be well, right? It's your baby. I have something to say about this just because I've seen it so many times. Mama's baby, daddy's maybe. If the child is yours by all means take care of him or her. If you are in the child support system, there are some things that you need to take into consideration.

NUMBER ONE: Is this child yours?

Do you want to continue to take care of a child that may not be yours for 18+ years?

Get a DNA test. If you don't then you're a duck. #quack #quack This is one of those things that you can't let emotions get the best of you. You can love the child and he or she not be yours biologically but child support usually means you're no longer with the other parent. Why on earth would you sign up for support payments on a child that isn't yours? I'm not saying don't do anything for them, I'm saying why would you allow a court order to be put in place? What about your future family? What about when you have children of your own? I'm just asking. It's a business decision not an emotional one.

1. Do you pay cash outside of the system?
   Why?

2. What happens when you're out of work because of accident, lay off or sickness?

This is what has people getting locked up left and right waiting on a purge. Someone else has to come bail you out because all the money you were giving, if any, wasn't going through their system or you just didn't handle your business.

If you are behind on child support EVERY DIME needs to go through the system. Birthday's and Christmas don't matter. Yes, I said it. I've seen people do some dumb mess just to provide gifts then they end up in jail now the child has no parent or presents.

Doesn't it make more sense to pay everything you can through the system to cover yourself in case you're ever out of work? If little man or miss needs braces or wants some J's give the primary parent the money for it if you have it. Just run it through child support. I don't care who doesn't agree with me on this I've seen people who are tens of thousands behind in child support go buy school clothes. Ok now idiot. When you're in jail for a purge now someone else will have to take care of your business and your kids for you. Way to go.

There is nothing wrong with asking for a modification when your circumstances change. Just like custodial parents ask for more as the child's needs change You can ask for adjustments as well. Child support has to take both parents income into consideration. I think I said it before, file for visitation rights. Have your rights on paper. That might hold down some confusion or at least give you a leg to stand on if things aren't working out.

Another gateway to prison is when the person you are with is used to your old ways and won't let you change. They don't have the patience or don't accept your new choices that help you to remain free. Sometimes, it behooves you to drop that bad habit. Someone yapping constantly in your ear about what you used to do that kept your pocket fat but also put your freedom in jeopardy, generally doesn't mean you any good. Make the executive decision to excuse that person from current circle and go build your free, peaceful, prosperous future.

17 No, Thank You!

Being "about that life" was never a problem until I tried to make a change. Certain car insurance companies wouldn't accept me as a client. I've paid a direct sales financial company for my life insurance every month for the past 18 years. They would not allow me to sell their products because of my record. And it doesn't matter that my record doesn't reflect anything fraudulent or dishonest. So it's not only brick and mortar jobs that pose a problem.

There were other times when having a criminal background made things difficult. I couldn't chaperone field trips or even eat lunch with my children at school unless it was in the front office. I filled out the volunteer form just to see what would happen. Another reason was because my daughter asked me to. She wanted me to go to a theme park field trip with her class. I was denied. When I called to ask why I was denied the lady said, "ma'am I think you know why".

I got involved with a direct sales company where I sell high fashion jewelry as an independent consultant. I am grateful that no one ever asked about my background because that doesn't even matter when I'm out being fabulous! At the moment I lead a growing team of over 40 consultants, I get mentored by the best, and I am constantly exposed to the next level of greatness! This is something that I would not have been achieving at a regular job. The personal development is nothing is less than phenomenal! I find that regular jobs like to keep you in a box, I was not made to fit in, I was made to stand out!

On one job I was a billing specialist but I also understood database administration very well because I excelled in it in technical school. An opportunity arose for me to help write scripts for our accounting program that the company would pay consultants thousands of dollars to come in and do. but my supervisor told me to just stick to my billing. (side eye) I was so frustrated with not being allowed to grow.

One thing that I love about direct sales and MLM (multi-level marketing) is the personal development and mindset shifts that take place. Find one that you're passionate about and go learn as much as you can. Do it as a side gig or build it up to full-time. It's great not to have to reinvent the wheel! The products are only a part of it. It works if you do. Grow your network. It is true that your network equals your net worth. I know you've heard someone say before it's not what you know it's who you know. I have done so much networking with my direct sales company and met so many people that it is helping me moving forward in all of my new endeavors.

  Entrepreneurship isn't for everyone but it is a viable option when no one will give you a real chance. Create something for yourself. There are minimum wage or low paying jobs but it's what you do with them while you're working that can make you or break you.

All those other no's put me right where I am supposed to be. So thank you to all those people who told me NO.

18 I got the keys, the keys, the keys

I hear many convicted felons saying they can't find housing because when going to rent somewhere they do background checks and are denied based on having a felony. Well, no one is going to tell you that you can't purchase your own home and it's not as hard as you may think. Instead of thinking "woe is me", think of it as your destiny pushing you into what you really need to be doing and then go do something about it!

There are all kinds of first-time buyer programs and I'm sure there are many other programs that help you purchase a home, condo or townhouse. Do some research and find out what it takes to qualify. Many of these programs will make you jump through some hoops get your ducks in a row and do it! It will be worth it.

You'll find out that the differences between owning your place and renting are both challenging and beneficial.

Imagine building equity and wealth just from paying your mortgage. Renting is just throwing money out the window. Do it while you have to but keep your eyes on the prize.

You won't be tied down to one place if you own your property. Here is your opportunity to be an entrepreneur. If you have to move for any reason you could always sell your place, or rent it out now you're a landlord/ real estate investor! You can rent to section 8 while you go off and continue to be great. Who told you that you can't do these things? You absolutely can. Stop thinking everything is out of reach for you. All you have to do is research and educate yourself. Sometimes you must be willing to forgo short-term comfort for long-term goal. Meaning if you have to work all day then study all evening for a little while then do it.

Change your surroundings from people who aren't doing anything different than what you may be used to. People look at folks who own their homes as rich or think that they did something special and unattainable. I heard somewhere that you can't want to be rich and dislike rich people.

The only difference between you and people who own their homes are choices. They made a choice to invest and others choose to rent. The money will go out all the same. Sometimes you get more for your money or spend less on a mortgage than you do for rent.

I know many people want regular jobs, just to go somewhere clock in and earn a paycheck. I will admit that there is some comfort in that. We all have greatness in us and sometimes these adversities put us in a place where we have to make things happen.

My husband and I purchased our own home two years after I was released from prison. It took two average incomes and creating good credit to accomplish this. I was waiting tables and he was hanging billboards. We had a small wedding and a nice reception catered by family and used all of the cash received from wedding gifts to clear up pre-marital bills. So we didn't start our journey with debt.

19 Broke, Busted, & Disgusted?

If your finances are just in shambles, and your credit is a mess, you have way too many things to pay off with the money that you're earning, add restitution, child-support, and everybody looking at you to see if you're going to mess up again then you might have to take some drastic steps.

One option could be checking into bankruptcy. Some people think that it's a bad thing, I think it's a fresh start for people who need it. Sometimes it works out better for a person to pay an attorney to handle their bankruptcy case than to pay off the years of neglected debts and mess ups. If you think about it the bad debt will still be on your credit file for 7 to 10 years anyway wouldn't you rather have a fresh start? Once someone files bankruptcy, they can begin rebuilding credit. I stress good credit not so much for people to go out and abuse it but to be a good steward over it and use it in a way to live a comfortable life and build wealth. This is one of those things that you have to educate yourself on before making a decision. *Disclaimer I am not an attorney or tax professional and I'm not giving you legal or tax advice. You should know though that certain debts can't be discharged or are extremely difficult to discharge in bankruptcy like child support, student loans, traffic tickets, and certain taxes. However, with other unsecured or consumer debt wiped away it can give you the leeway to pay off some of these non-dischargeable debts.

20 Seven Things I Wish I Knew as a Juvenile

1) NOT to plead guilty to everything.

   I was horrified looking at a printout of my juvenile record. I see that I plead guilty to everything!

2) NEGOTIATE plea deals. ASK for what you want.

3) Take school more serious.

   I was a serial truant since 7th grade. I went to school when I wanted to and still managed to pass. Imagine if I would have applied myself back then.

4) LISTEN to wise counsel.

   Teens think they know everything. It's smarter to learn from other people's mistakes.

5) Some parents know what they're talking about.

Some of them. They do the best they can. Parenting doesn't come with a manual.

6) Speak up THEN if someone takes advantage of you.

I think this is why there are so many messed up adults. We carry unnecessary burdens all our lives which eventually affects the way we live.

7) Your "friends" don't always have your best interest at heart.

I was warned. There was destruction.

21 Re-Entry Action List

- Have your family relationships changed?
- Do you have a plan? What is it?
- Things have changed even if you were only gone for a short time.
- Technology has changed.
- Be open minded, humble and ready to learn.
- If you don't have a positive support system in your family, reach out to a church or community organization.
- Keep it moving in a positive direction.
- Change your friends and surroundings for the better.

Stay in Touch & Support

- Looking for an additional stream income?
- Want to join a winning team?
- Do you like FREE accessories?

You can find my accessories website here: **http://bit.ly/toniaqua**

For booking and bulk orders email:
info@toniaquarterman.com
Or go to
www.toniaquarterman.com

Become a book sponsor!

The NOW WHAT? Is a real question many people have when returning to society. My goal is to impact as many people as possible and I need your help! Will you be willing to help me put this book into the hands of returning citizens who are in re-entry programs, work release centers and domestic violence shelters to inspire and reassure them that success is possible regardless of their past. I can only do this with your help. Sponsor one book or many. You can even pledge a small amount every month. Your generosity is appreciated. Your statement will say MQTQ Enterprises LLC.

www.toniaquarterman.com Click Donate or **www.paypal.me/toniaq**

Coming Soon!

From RAP SHEETS TO RESUMES
written by
Tonia Quarterman

Keep Your Hands To Yourself

TONIA QUARTERMAN

Notes

Action Plan

Affirmations

Contacts

To Do List

The Ex-Con Factor

The Ex-Con Factor

The Ex-Con Factor